Basic Floral Design

...Arrangements you can do yourself.

Inquiries should be addressed to:

The John Henry Company
P.O. Box 17099
5800 W. Grand River Ave.
Lansing, MI 48901

Library of Congress
Catalog Card Number: 97-70797
ISBN 0-9630431-3-7

Published, printed and distributed by
The John Henry Company
Lansing, MI

Table of Contents

Introduction 5

Basic Floral Design was developed to provide a basic understanding of the world of flowers as it relates to the art of floral design. The book will guide you through the creation of six popular arrangement styles. Each style is featured in it's own section, highlighted with colorful photographs, illustrations, and step-by-step instruction.

By using Basic Floral Design, you will learn about where flowers are grown, their seasonal availability, and how individual flower varieties can be used in different arrangement styles.

Finally, Basic Floral Design is filled with many valuable tips on do-it-yourself floral design, including fresh flower care and handling, flower identification, required tools and supplies, and basic floral design principles.

Basic Floral Design welcomes you to the world of flowers!

The World of Flowers

Where Do Commercial Flowers Come From?

While virtually every country on earth produces some sort of floral product for domestic consumption, there are approximately 20 countries which produce significant amounts of cut flowers and/or foliages for export. Four countries — Holland, Colombia, Italy and Israel — account for a major portion of this supply. Several other countries vying for attention in the cut flower export market include Kenya, Spain, France, the United States, South Africa, Mexico and Jamaica.

The world flower market has experienced many dramatic changes in the past 15 to 20 years. These changes are due to not one, but several factors. An increase in floral air transportation has allowed flowers to be delivered to any global destination within several hours or, at most, a few short days. New production areas, particularly in developing Third World countries, have increased the total acres in flower production worldwide. Advances in crop selection and cultivation practices which promote production efficiency have dramatically increased cut flower supplies on a year-round basis.

Colombia, which first entered the cut flower scene about 20 years ago with U.S.-based capital and expertise, has grown into a leading cut flower exporter. Almost 80 percent of Colombia's cut flowers are exported to the United States. Low costs for land, labor, and energy have helped Colombia become a force in today's global market.

Kenya has begun to develop into a major supplier of cut flowers. At this time, Kenyan exports are primarily bound for Europe with only a small percentage entering the United States. As with Colombia, costs for energy, land, and labor are low, allowing Kenya to become a fierce competitor for a share of the market.

Jamaica, a new contender in the world's flower market, began exporting several years ago, with the majority of its flowers coming to the United States and Canada. The island's tropical climate has given the world market another source for such field grown exotics as heliconia, ginger and anthurium. Jamaican growers also specialize in greenhouse grown roses and gerbera daisies.

Another new country in the cut flower market is Mexico. Having entered the marketplace in the early eighties, the Mexican market share has continued to grow. The majority of its cut flower crop is being exported to the United States and Canada. Due to its relatively close location, Mexico may vie with Colombia as a major supplier to the United States in the next few years.

Exports do not necessarily coincide with production. The United States, for example, is a major production source of floral crops; however, very little product is exported due to the amount of domestic consumption.

The countries which import the greatest number of floral products are Germany, the United States, France, Switzerland, Holland, Great Britain, Austria, Belgium/Luxembourg and Sweden. Holland is the major supplying country to all importing countries, except itself and the United States. For instance, in recent years a major portion of Holland's exports were shipped to Germany, France and Great Britain. Holland receives most of its imports from Israel, while the United States imports many cut flowers from Colombia.

Every country favors different flowers in different proportions, and consumption varies with availability and seasonality. However, on a worldwide basis, the greatest production is in carnations, roses and chrysanthemums. In the United States, the greatest production of cut flowers is in gladioli, chrysanthemums, carnations and roses.

Most countries produce a wide variety of flowers for domestic consumption; however, they may become better known as sources for certain products which they export. While the following list is by no means complete, it is an indication of some of the cut floral crops produced and/or sold by significant exporting countries.

Country	Known For
Holland	Roses, Carnations, Chrysanthemums, Freesia, Gerberas, Tulips, Lilies, Irises, Cymbidiums, Alstroemeria
Colombia	Carnations, Chrysanthemums, Roses, Gypsophila, Alstroemeria
Israel	Spray Carnations, Roses, Gerberas, Gypsophila, Greens, Liatris
Italy	Carnations, Roses, Greens
France	Chrysanthemums, Gladioli, Lilacs, Lilies, Ranunculus, Acacia, Roses, Anemones, Novelty Carnations, Tulips
Spain	Carnations, Roses, Chrysanthemums, Gladioli, Bird-of-Paradise
Kenya	Carnations, Plumosa, Liatris, Star of Bethlehem, Chrysanthemums, Bells of Ireland, Alstroemeria
United States	Gladioli, Chrysanthemums, Roses, Carnations, Anthuriums, Orchids, Leatherleaf Fern
South Africa	Proteas, Liatris, Chrysanthemums, Amaryllis, Carnations, Anthuriums, Roses, Cymbidium Orchids, Alstroemeria, Star of Bethlehem
Singapore	Orchids — Dendrobium, Vanda, Arachnis, Oncidium
Australia	Banksia, Cymbidium Orchids, Kangaroo Paws
Ivory Coast	Ornamental Pineapples, Heliconia, Ginger, Orchids

| Jamaica | Anthuriums, Heliconia, Ginger, Orchid species, Roses, Gerberas |
| Mexico | Roses, Carnations, Tuberoses, Statice, Gypsophila, Bird-of-Paradise, Ginger |

Supplies of major crops such as roses, carnations and mums are available on a year-round basis. Because they are produced by so many countries, a shortage of production in one area due to weather or other factors may temporarily affect prices, but not necessarily drastically affect supplies.

Some crops, however, may be produced in a few selected areas, so that when a crop is adversely affected by weather or other conditions, supplies may be severely reduced and prices may climb drastically. For example, unseasonably cold, wet weather in Florida can affect the quality and supplies of gladioli, leatherleaf fern and gypsophila for the United States. While imported supplies may be available, they cannot always compensate for shortages.

Seasonal availability is dependent on a plant's natural growing cycle. While many crops that used to be seasonal have now been bred to become year-round crops, some plants are still limited to natural cycles. This is particularly true of crops that are raised outside a greenhouse, where the environment cannot be controlled to any large degree.

Year-round availability of some crops is aided by the fact that the northern and southern hemispheres have opposite seasons. When it is winter in the northern hemisphere, it is summer in the southern hemisphere. Because summer weather conditions are generally more favorable for growing, production in the two hemispheres at opposite times of the year is able to balance supplies. Currently, the major flower-producing countries are in the northern hemisphere, but countries in the other half of the world are becoming increasingly important.

Flowers are harvested from growing fields, such as these, for worldwide distribution.

Photo courtesy of R. Kent Kimmins

Cut flowers and foliages are transported to market in many ways, but the most common carriers are trucks and planes. The greater the distance, the more likely that air transportation will be necessary. Unfortunately, air cargo space is somewhat expensive and can be limited. Once harvested, floral products are generally taken to central distribution points such as an auction or a transportation depot, and then redistributed to wholesalers and retailers around the globe.

Trucks are generally the mode of transport for flowers between most European countries. Within the United States, both air and land transportation are used to move products, with some major trucking lines specializing in the transfer of cut flowers and greens. While some growers in the U.S. do ship directly to retailers, the general path of distribution is shipment from the grower to a floral wholesaler, and then redistribution to retailers. Large multi-location grocery stores or retail florists and cooperative buying associations may purchase directly from growers, have the products delivered to a central receiving point, and then redistribute directly to retail outlets.

Where Flowers Come From

CENTERS OF FLOWER PRODUCTION
WESTERN HEMISPHERE

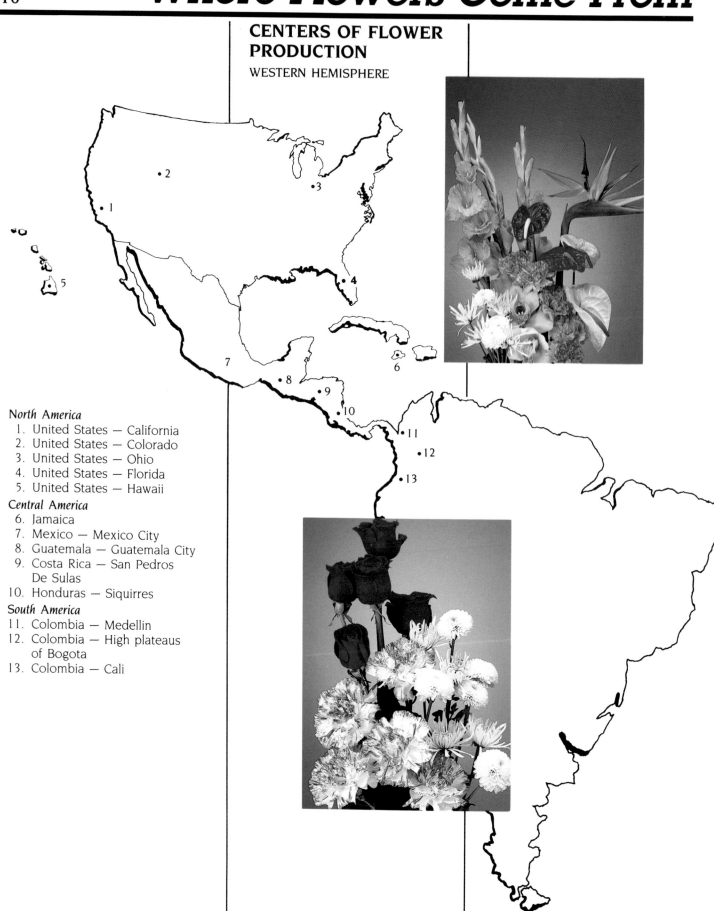

North America
1. United States — California
2. United States — Colorado
3. United States — Ohio
4. United States — Florida
5. United States — Hawaii

Central America
6. Jamaica
7. Mexico — Mexico City
8. Guatemala — Guatemala City
9. Costa Rica — San Pedros De Sulas
10. Honduras — Siquirres

South America
11. Colombia — Medellin
12. Colombia — High plateaus of Bogota
13. Colombia — Cali

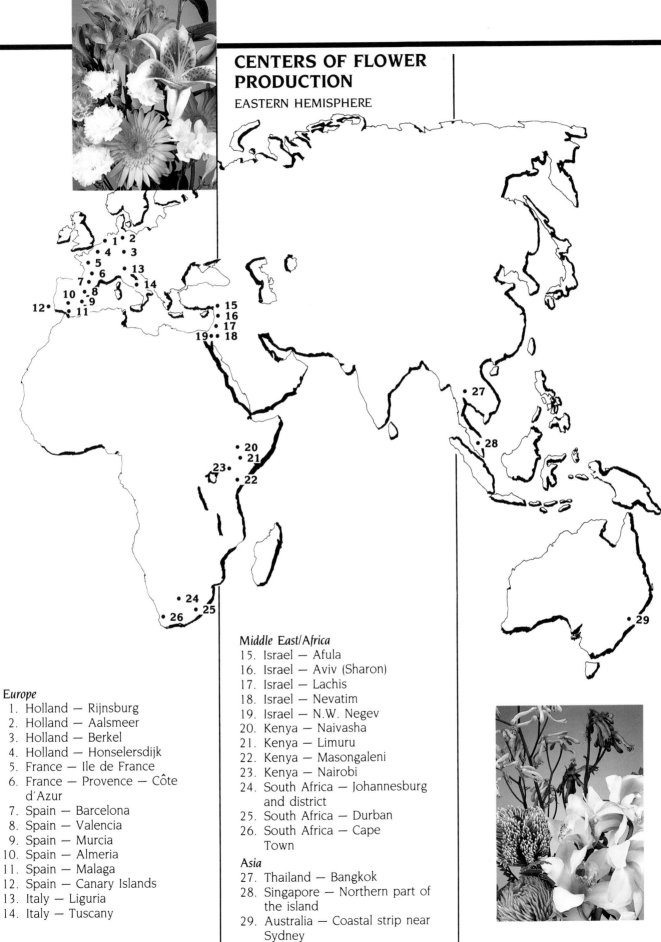

CENTERS OF FLOWER PRODUCTION
EASTERN HEMISPHERE

Europe
1. Holland — Rijnsburg
2. Holland — Aalsmeer
3. Holland — Berkel
4. Holland — Honselersdijk
5. France — Ile de France
6. France — Provence — Côte d'Azur
7. Spain — Barcelona
8. Spain — Valencia
9. Spain — Murcia
10. Spain — Almeria
11. Spain — Malaga
12. Spain — Canary Islands
13. Italy — Liguria
14. Italy — Tuscany

Middle East/Africa
15. Israel — Afula
16. Israel — Aviv (Sharon)
17. Israel — Lachis
18. Israel — Nevatim
19. Israel — N.W. Negev
20. Kenya — Naivasha
21. Kenya — Limuru
22. Kenya — Masongaleni
23. Kenya — Nairobi
24. South Africa — Johannesburg and district
25. South Africa — Durban
26. South Africa — Cape Town

Asia
27. Thailand — Bangkok
28. Singapore — Northern part of the island
29. Australia — Coastal strip near Sydney

To ensure the lasting quality of the flowers you purchase, use the following basic steps as a guide.

1. Be sure a flower care tag is included each time you purchase flowers to remind you of proper care.

2. Look for a packet of floral preservative. If one has not been included with your purchase, ask for it. Floral preservative prolongs the vase life of flowers if used properly. Follow the instructions listed on the packet carefully.

3. Select the proper container to use with the flowers you have purchased. The container should have a large enough mouth to hold the flowers securely but not too tightly. It should provide an ample reservoir of water because flowers in the home will lose their natural moisture and take up water rapidly.

4. Once you get your flower purchase home, carefully remove all packaging materials including any water tubes which may have been placed on the individual stems. Handle these flowers as little as possible to avoid bruising or crushing.

5. Loose flower stems should be cut about one inch from the bottom, underwater. Remove any foliage that will be below the water line before placing them in a vase of preservative solution. Water should be warm (110°F) to mix the preservative. To judge this temperature, run water over the back of your hand. When the water feels like a nice warm bath, it is ready for flowers.

6. Do not place flowers in direct sunlight, near sources of heat or cold, or in a draft. These conditions can cause premature wilting of flowers and dramatically shorten vase life.

7. If flowers have been placed in a vase, remove blossoms as they die in order to preserve the fresher flowers. If flowers have been placed in a container arrangement, pick off dying blooms and foliage. This will not only improve the appearance of the arrangement, but will remove decaying material in order to preserve the fresher flowers.

8. Flower stems which have been placed in a vase of water should be removed and recut underwater every four to five days to promote water uptake; change preservative solution (warm water) and clean the container at the same time. Flowers that have been arranged in a container should have warm preservative solution added daily. Make sure the arranging foam does not dry out.

Other tips for success:

1. Flowers should not be placed near fruit or vegetables or placed in the refrigerator next to these items. Many varieties of fruits and vegetables give off ethylene gas, which can adversely affect flower life.

2. Whenever possible, move flowers to a cool location at night. While a cool room is recommended, if storing in a refrigerator is your only option, make sure it is clear of fruits and vegetables. Place the flowers (in their container) in a plastic bag with some wet paper toweling in the bag. Refrigerators can actually dehydrate flowers because they do not provide humidity. Flowers should be stored in the highest part of the refrigerator to protect them from too much chilling. Remove the flowers from the bag the next day.

3. Vases used for flowers and greens should be thoroughly cleaned before the next use. Soapy detergents and hot water are the best. The sides should be cleaned to remove any clinging particles or bacterial build-up. They should be thoroughly rinsed with very hot water and then dried.

4. Flowers have varying vase lives. Ask when making your purchase how long the varieties will last under proper care conditions. If you know at the outset, you will not be disappointed if the flowers die in a short period of time.

5. If you purchase flowers to place in container arrangements, other than loosely in a vase, be sure you place them in a clean bucket with floral preservative until you are ready to use them. Follow the directions listed on page 12.

6. Look for and purchase the freshest flowers available.

7. Foliage materials should be cared for and handled in the same manner as fresh flowers.

8. For additional foliage material, cut discreetly from plants you already have at home. Place in water as described before.

9. Do not expose flowers to freezing temperatures (including freezing wind chills). Exposed flowers will turn transparent and die.

By following the basic flower care and handling steps listed on pages 12 and 13, you can enjoy the maximum vase life of the flowers and the natural beauty they bring to any occasion.

Flower Classifications

Flowers and foliages have distinct shapes which give interest to floral arrangements. There are four classifications of flowers and foliages. Some fit into several categories, depending upon the degree of openness or how the materials will be used in a composition.

You do not have to have all four types of flowers in every floral arrangement; any combination of the four or any one group may be used. The four shapes can give you a guideline to designing. Line material should be placed first to create the size and shape of the design. Add form material to give the design interest and a focal point; mass material to give the design weight and bulk; and filler material to make the design full and complete.

Delphinium is a good example of a line flower.

A hybrid lily is a good example of a form flower.

An aster is a good example of a mass flower.

Gypsophila is a good example of a filler flower.

Line Material — Line materials are generally erect, tall spikes of blossoms with florets blooming along the stem. They give a feeling of length and create linear pattern. They are generally used to establish the outline of the floral design, and also determine the size of the arrangement. Examples of line materials are bells-of-ireland, delphinium, gladioli, heather, liatris, snapdragons, stock, pussywillow, scotch broom and ti leaves.

Form Material — Form materials have distinctive shapes. Space should be maintained between them if they are to remain individuals. Form materials are used at the focal point and are beautiful when designed alone. Some which have strong outlines can be used as silhouette blossoms on the outer edge of the arrangement. Examples of form flowers are anthurium, bird of paradise, gerbera daisies, iris, lilies, protea, orchids, tulips, caladium foliage and croton foliage.

Mass Material — Mass materials have single stems with one solid head. Their main function is to give the arrangement weight and bulk; they are generally used toward the focal point. When used alone in an arrangement, buds or smaller blossoms are placed at the outer edges. The height and depth should be varied so that each one shows its individual shape. Examples of mass materials are asters, carnations, chrysanthemums, roses, galax leaves, and calathea.

Filler Material — Filler materials are used to "fill in" and "soften" arrangements. They are used in the background and generally are low in the arrangement; they add depth. Be careful to avoid the tendency to add too much filler material, because this will detract from the arrangement. Examples of filler materials are gypsophila, statice, waxflower, leatherleaf, and huckleberry.

The Fresh Flower Identification Chart on pages 15-17 identifies many of the most popular flowers and foliages and indicates their availability.

     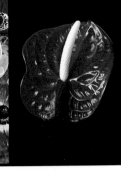

ACACIA
Available October through March in yellow.

AGAPANTHUS
Available May through August in white, blue and lavender.

ALSTROEMERIA
Available year-round in shades of pink, red, yellow, lavender and white.●

AMARYLLIS
Available year-round in shades of red, pink, orange, white and bicolors.●

ANEMONE
Available October through May in shades of red, pink, white, and blue.●

ANTHURIUM
Available year-round in red, white, pink, orange and variegated shades.●

ASTER
Available June through September in shades of white, pink, lavender and purple.

ASTILBE
Available March through December in pink, white and burgundy.

BIRD OF PARADISE
Available September to June in orange/blue.

BOUVARDIA
Available year-round in shades of red, orange, white and pink.●

CALLA LILY
Available March through June in white, pink and yellow.●

CARNATION
Available year-round in shades of white, pink, peach, red, yellow and variegated varieties.●

MINIATURE CARNATION
Available year-round in shades of white, pink, peach, red, yellow and variegated varieties.●

CORNFLOWER
Available April through September in blue, pink and white.

DAFFODIL
Available November through April in yellow and white.●

CHRYSANTHEMUM
Available year-round in shades of bronze, gold, lavender, yellow and white.

FUJI CHRYSANTHEMUM
Available year-round in white, yellow and lavender.

POMPON CHRYSANTHEMUM
Available year-round in shades of bronze, gold, lavender, yellow and white.

DELPHINIUM
Available June through September in shades of blue, lavender, purple, pink and white.

EUPHORBIA
Available August through February in orange, yellow, red, pink, gold and white.●

FREESIA
Available year-round in shades of yellow, white, pink and lavender.●

GARDENIA
Available year-round in white.

FORSYTHIA
Available November through March in shades of yellow.

GERBERA DAISY
Available year-round in shades of pink, orange, red, white, yellow and bicolors.●

FRESH FLOWER IDENTIFICATION CHART

GLADIOLUS
Available year-round in shades of white, pink, red, yellow, peach, purple and bicolors.

MINIATURE GLADIOLUS
Available May through June in shades of white, red and pink. ●

GYPSOPHILA
Available year-round in white and pink.

HEATHER
Available November through March in rose, lavender and white.

HYACINTH
Available November through April in pink, white and purple.

IRIS
Available year-round in purple, yellow, white and blue. ●

LIATRIS
Available year-round in lavender and white.

LILAC
Available December through May in white, pink, lavender and purple. ●

LILY OF THE VALLEY
Available year-round in white.

RUBRUM LILY
Available year-round in shades of pink and white.

HYBRID LILY
Available year-round in shades of pink, white, yellow and orange.

DAISY
Available year-round in white and yellow.

NERINE LILY
Available year-round in shades of pink, white, red and orange.

CYMBIDIUM ORCHID
Available year-round in shades of pink, lavender, white, yellow and green. ●

DENDROBIUM ORCHID
Available year-round in shades of lavender, white, pink and bicolors. ●

CATTLEYA ORCHID
Available year-round in white, lavender and bicolors.

PHALAENOPSIS ORCHID
Available year-round in white and lavender.

PROTEA
Available year-round in shades of pink, green, yellow, orange and red depending on variety.

  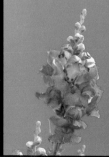   

RANUNCULUS
Available February through May in yellow, orange, red, pink and white.

ROSE
Available year-round in red, pink, yellow, white, peach and bicolors. ●

SPRAY ROSE
Available year-round in pink and orange. ●

SNAPDRAGON
Available year-round in white, pink, lavender and yellow.

STAR OF BETHLEHEM
Available year-round in white. ●

STEPHANOTIS
Available year-round in white.

GERMAN STATICE
Available year-round in white.

STATICE
Available year-round in shades of white, yellow, pink and purple.

TRITOMA
Available June through October in shades of red and yellow.

TULIP
Available November through May in shades of red, pink, yellow, orange, white and bicolors. ●

YARROW
Available July through September in yellow.

WAX FLOWER
Available December through May in pink and white.

BEAR GRASS
Available year-round in green.

CAMELLIA
Available year-round in dark green.

EUCALYPTUS
Available year-round in blue-green.

FERN
Available year-round in celery green.

GALAX
Available year-round in dark green.

HUCKLEBERRY
Available year-round in deep green.

IVY
Available year-round in deep green and variegated varieties.

LEATHERLEAF
Available year-round in dark green.

MING FERN
Available year-round in bright green.

MYRTLE
Available October through March in green.

PALM
Available year-round in green.

PITTOSPORUM
Available year-round in green and variegated varieties.

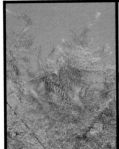

PLUMOSA
Available year-round in bright green.

SALAL
Available year-round in dark green.

ITALIAN RUSCUS
Available year-round in dark green.

SCOTCH BROOM
Available August through April in green.

SPRENGERI
Available year-round in green.

TREE FERN
Available year-round in green.

● Photos Courtesy of the Flower Council of Holland.

Design
Supplies

Vase Containers

Basic Containers

Basket Containers

Ceramic Containers

There are numerous floral design supplies available. The categories reviewed here are containers, basic mechanical supplies and tools. The design supplies featured on the following pages are generally available at craft and hobby stores, mass merchandisers and retail floral outlets. Many home accessory items you may already own are suitable for floral design projects.

Containers

The first element in floral design is choosing a proper container. Consider how the arrangement is going to be used, what occasion it is for and what types of flowers are going to be included. The container should be large enough to hold the materials without crowding and deep enough to hold sufficient water.

Vases come in a variety of sizes and shapes to accommodate several different design styles. Bud vases are usually taller with a narrow opening. Taller vases with wider openings allow for a dozen flowers to be arranged so that they can be viewed from one side or all the way around. Other shapes can be used for mixed arrangements. They lend themselves to more casual, freeform design styles. Vases are usually made of glass, ceramic or plastic.

Inexpensive, attractive everyday containers are used when the container will not be too visible or will be set inside a more decorative container. Low plastic containers, including compotes and footed bowls, are used for centerpieces and basket liners.

Baskets for floral design come in a wide variety of shapes and sizes, with and without liners and handles. They are made out of many different materials and can be painted, stained or left in a natural state. Baskets are often as inexpensive as utility containers, yet far more decorative, and they can be used for just about any occasion.

Ceramic containers come in a variety of shapes. Ceramic utility containers are similar to those made in plastic. Novelty containers, made with decorative accents or in special shapes, are used for baby, masculine, holidays or any floral design that might have special meaning. Be sure the novelty container is suitable for the occasion and has an opening large enough and positioned properly to make an effective design. Other ceramic containers include jardinieres, compotes, mugs and vases.

Tips on Selecting Containers

Size — visualize the completed arrangement. Size of the opening determines how many flowers will be needed to fill the container properly.

Shape — should flow with the arrangement to create harmony.

Style — should coordinate with the desired theme of the arrangement.

Texture — should complement the materials used in the design.

Color — can blend with a design or become part of the focal point. Decorator colors are an important consideration.

The physical stability and practicality of most arrangements lie in good mechanics. Common mechanical supplies include fresh floral foam, wire mesh netting, silk and dried foam, Styrofoam™, shredded Styrofoam™ and needlepoint holders.

Fresh Floral Foam

Floral foam comes in blocks which can be cut to the desired size. There are different types of foam for various needs.

To use floral foam, soak in water until thoroughly saturated. Do not try to force water into the foam, because air pockets may form in the center of the block. Soak floral foam prior to use. Floral preservatives should be added to the water, unless you are using a foam type which has preservatives already in it. Unused portions of blocks should be stored in water to be ready for future use, because the foam will dry out if left out of water.

In the container, floral foam should be positioned so that part of it extends above the container. Make sure there is room to add water. When arranging in floral foam, make sure flower stems are inserted securely. This allows for better stability and better water absorption. Water should be replenished in the container frequently. There are several different brands of floral foam you may try in your arrangements to see which one works best for you.

Wire Mesh Netting

"Chicken wire" is usually available in a 1-inch mesh. This size is more pliable and easier to use. It is most often used to provide extra stability over floral foam in heavy arrangements. To use, cut to fit over the foam in a container. When inserting flowers through the wire mesh, take care not to split or damage the stems.

Basic Mechanical Supplies

Silk and Dried Foam

Silk and dried foam is designed primarily for use with silk and dried materials, but it also has many other applications. It comes in blocks for permanent arrangements, sheets and form shapes for wreaths. Silk and dried foam securely grips stems, attaches to containers with glue and will not melt when spray paint is applied.

Styrofoam™

Styrofoam™, primarily used in display and sculpture work, can be cut and styled into any shape. It can also be used to secure heavier objects, like large silk plants, into pots. Styrofoam™ is rigid and sturdy.

Shredded, it can be used to fill larger containers. It must be packed tightly into the container in order to hold flowers securely. It can also be used as a filler base for floral foam. Fill the container and place the floral foam on top. Cover with wire mesh for extra protection against flower movement. Tape over the top to secure.

Needlepoint Holder

A flower "frog" is a metal-based object with needle-like prongs projecting up from the base. "Frogs" come in many shapes and sizes. Secure the holder to the container, then cut flower stems at an angle so the cut surface will lie flat on the base of the holder. Flower holders are best used for oriental style arrangements or in the bottom of a vase to help hold a mass of flowers in place.

Tools and Supplies

Basic Design Tools

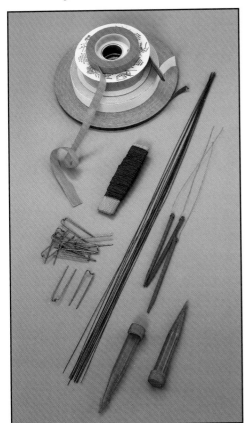

Basic Design Supplies

Use of the proper tools and supplies can make floral design easy. Tools necessary for basic design include design knife, wire snips, ribbon shears, and glue gun. Supplies include floral tape, waterproof tape, double-sided tape, floral adhesives, wire, picks, water tubes and greening pins.

Knife

A knife is the most important tool a designer owns. A good knife is essential, since **all flower stems must be cut before being placed into an arrangement**. Personal preference is the rule; choose one which feels comfortable in the hand. A folding knife is the most popular choice—it can be sharpened and then closed so it can be carried without the danger of hurting someone.

First attempts at using a floral knife can result in cut thumbs. To avoid this, grasp the flower stem in one hand. Hold the knife in the palm of the other hand and guide the blade edge along the stem without using your thumb for support. While cutting, pull the stem upwards to help relieve the pressure of cutting on the stem. After a small amount of practice, using a floral knife will become second nature.

Wire Snips

Wire snips are helpful when cutting stubborn items which cannot be cut with a floral knife. There are different types of snips with different uses. Utility snips are used for shortening wire lengths, cutting artificial stems and sturdy foliage branches, and other day-to-day needs. They can cut through a large quantity of wire easily. Wire cutters are primarily used to cut through heavy gauge wire. They are sturdier and can cut wire mesh netting or thick artificial stems.

Ribbon Shears

Ribbon shears are useful for items which do not require a cut through metal. They are primarily used for cutting ribbon, trimming foliage or any other situation where a clean, sharp edge is needed. Like floral knives, ribbon shears should be kept sharp.

Glue Gun

The hot glue gun has become one of the most versatile and often-used tools in flower arranging, revolutionizing and shortening many traditional hand operations. It is excellent to use for design activities such as securing foam into containers, adding trim or building stacked containers.

Heat glue gun before use. When it is hot, glue should ooze out at the touch of the trigger. Use glue as needed. When finished, release the trigger and move the gun in a circular motion, ending with an upward movement to break off the glue. This will help prevent glue from "stringing" on the workbench.

Be very careful in using the glue gun, because glue becomes very hot and can burn. A first-aid kit readily at hand is a wise precaution.

The glue comes in the form of sticks that are inserted into the gun. Use glue sticks that have been specifically recommended by the manufacturer of your gun. This will prevent clogging and unexpected malfunctions. Use your individual creativity to find numerous and varied uses for the glue gun and to discover the many ways this tool can save time.

Floral Tape

Floral tape is a self-sealing wrap for covering stems or wires. It is most often used to wrap stems which have been wired. It is also used for fastening novelty items to picks for insertion into arrangements.

Waterproof Tape

This type of tape is most often used to hold floral foam in a container. It is normally criss-crossed across the foam to four points on the container and secured. It will adhere to clean, dry surfaces only. If the tape will not adhere, wash the container in hot, soapy water and dry. Waterproof tape usually comes in 2 widths: wide for larger containers and narrow for smaller, more delicate designs. It is available in green, white and clear.

Double-sided Tape

This type of tape is clear and has adhesive on both sides. It can be used to secure ribbon, attach trims to tables, hold foil on pots or in any project that would involve securing the elements invisibly.

Floral Adhesives

There are several adhesives used in floral design. A clay-like adhesive is available to secure Styrofoam™ or hold fruit, flower frogs or other objects in place. Cut the desired length from the roll and place on object to be secured. Remove paper backing and position object in place. Don't handle it a lot—it will lose its effectiveness.

Aerosol spray glues are effective when working with small areas. They also dry quickly. Be aware that the cans can become plugged. To help prevent this, press the spray button all the way down and press the tip when using. After using, turn can upside down and press the tip until the spray is free of adhesive.

Liquid brush-on glues are useful when covering larger areas. They can be used to secure ribbon and trim materials. These glues have a tendency to self-glue the top closed. To help prevent this, apply Vaseline® to the rim of the can when first opened or spray the rim with aerosol hand cleaner after each use.

Hot pan melt glue is similar to glue applied with a glue gun (see page 21). Glue blocks or chips are melted in a pan, creating a mass of hot glue. Items are dipped into it and placed in the desired position. This allows you the freedom from constantly needing to pick up the glue gun when many items need to be positioned. Again, caution must be advised, because the glue is extremely hot and can cause burns.

Wire

Wire is a staple of floral design. It comes in many gauges and can be used to curve a stem, straighten a crooked stem or strengthen a weak stem. It also has many other applications. Paddle wire is also available for use when longer lengths are required. Specific information on wire can be found on page 36.

Picks

Two different types of floral picks are available for design. Wooden picks come in various lengths and have pointed ends with a fine wire attached at the opposite end. These picks have a variety of uses, including inserting novelty trim into arrangements, lengthening a stem and inserting flowers. Steel picks are used mainly to secure silk and dried materials in designs. A special pick machine is required to secure the pick on the stem. These picks are very sharp, and care should be taken when using them.

Water Tubes

These are rubber-capped plastic tubes which hold water. Placing a short-stemmed flower, like an orchid, into a water tube will allow it to be designed into an arrangement more effectively than the natural stem would allow. Water tubes can be inserted directly into floral foam or taped to wooden picks for additional height. Care should be taken to camouflage them in arrangements. Water tubes can also be used to place fresh flowers into green planters for colorful accents. Water should be added to the tube on a daily basis.

Greening Pins

Greening pins resemble hairpins with flat tops.. They are used to attach moss or foliage to designs, container bases, etc. They are especially useful when working with Styrofoam™ or silk and dried foam. To use, place material to be pinned on the foam surface and push the pin down through material to secure.

Design
Principles

Color is a key element of floral design. It can be an effective accent for interior designs, seasonal holidays and parties. When working with interior design, use color to make your arrangement a decorative accent. Seasonal and holiday occasions have changing color themes. Pastels for spring, brighter mixed colors for summer, yellows, bronzes and oranges for fall and whites and blues for winter represent the seasonal color changes. Holiday color changes include red, pink and white for Valentine's Day, pastel for Easter and Mother's Day, earthtones for Father's Day and Thanksgiving, green for St. Patrick's Day and red and green for Christmas.

To better understand the use of color in design, it is important to understand the four different color schemes.

This floral arrangement is an example of complementary color.

The Monochromatic Color Scheme

Monochromatic design is achieved by the use of a single color. Interest is developed by the selection of various intensities of that color. An arrangement of pale pink roses and deep pink carnations is more interesting than the same arrangement with both flowers in the same shade of pink. The design at left using yellow lilies, freesia, button pompons and a fuji mum exemplifies the monochromatic color scheme. The rule for working with monochromatic colors is simple: stay with one color.

The Complementary Color Scheme

The use of color opposites develops the complementary color scheme. It constitutes a harmony which offers the strongest possible contrast. With the use of a color wheel (see page 26), you can easily determine complementary colors. First pick the color you want to be the primary, or dominant, color in your design. The color directly opposite on the color wheel is the complementary color. Flowers in red and green, yellow and violet, and blue and orange are all complementary to each other. To achieve a correct complement, equal intensities of the colors should always be combined. It is proper to add an accent of a

This floral arrangement is an example of monochromatic color.

different tone of the flower color in the focal area of the arrangement. The design on page 24 using yellow pompons, lavender pompons and miniature carnations and purple statice exemplifies the use of complementary colors.

The Analogous Color Scheme

Analogous colors are those which lie adjacent to each other on the color wheel within a 90-degree angle. Some of the richest and most effective color combinations are created with the use of analogous colors. Analogous is warm color because each color contains some of the same primary hue. Yellow-orange and yellow, as well as yellow-green and yellow, are analogous because each contains yellow. The design (upper right) using orange lilies, miniature carnations, sweetheart roses and yellow fuji pompons exemplifies the use of analogous color.

The Triadic Color Scheme

A color triad is made from three colors the same distance apart on the color wheel. Looking at the color wheel, you will find that red, yellow and blue form a triad. Color triads are difficult to work with, because they become harsh and gaudy unless great care is used in the selection of flowers and colors. Correctly used, however, a triad can develop a rich dramatic effect. The design (lower right) using peach gerbera daisies, sonia roses, lavender freesia and purple statice exemplifies the use of triadic color. In this case, the rich green foliage becomes the third color of the arrangement.

Color Tints

Flowers may not always be available in the colors needed to complete a design. Whenever possible, use a color scheme that allows the use of natural color. If this is not possible, the use of coloring products may become necessary. There are many coloring techniques, including spray paint, floral tint sprays and floral dip dyes. Whichever technique you choose, the key is to make the flowers appear as natural as possible.

This floral arrangement is an example of analogous color.

This floral arrangement is an example of triadic color.

The Color Wheel

Demonstrates the Relationship of Color in the Spectrum

Color is the most important element of flower selection in floral design. Understanding color will allow you to achieve the best creation possible. The color wheel is a good tool for successful floral design: keep this wheel handy when selecting flowers for your designs.

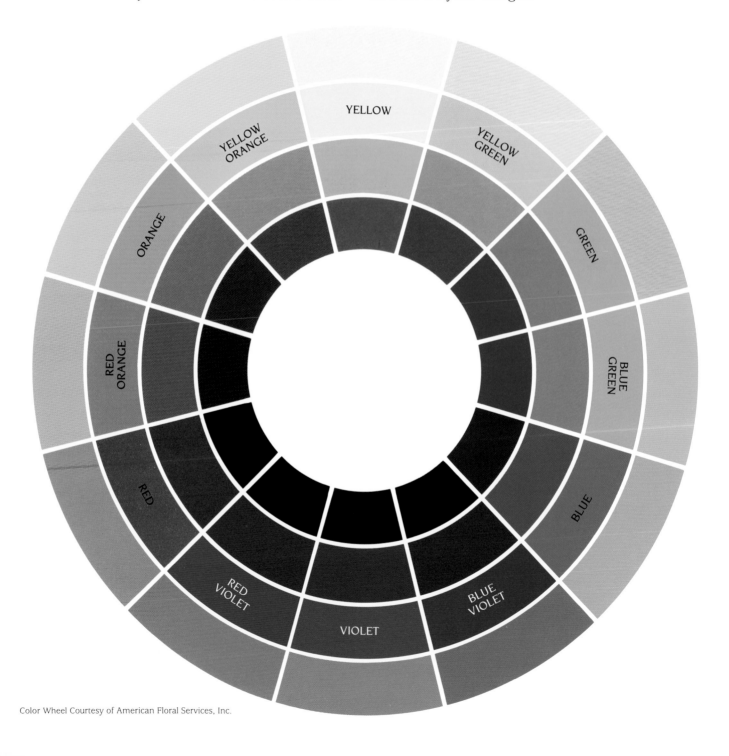

YELLOW

YELLOW ORANGE

YELLOW GREEN

ORANGE

GREEN

RED ORANGE

BLUE GREEN

RED

BLUE

RED VIOLET

BLUE VIOLET

VIOLET

Color Wheel Courtesy of American Floral Services, Inc.

Arrangement and Composition

A floral arrangement is a three-dimensional picture having height, width and depth. It is composed by planning groups of items, such as flowers, foliages, containers, accessories, and backgrounds, which have a pleasing relationship to each other. All parts relate so that they blend together.

An important part of floral design is composition—how and where the arrangement will be used. Individual preference and current trends often dictate suitability of an arrangement. You should compose the type of arrangement best suited for the occasion.

Questions to ask yourself when composing an arrangement:

1. For what occasion will the arrangement be used?
2. From what distance will the arrangement be seen?
3. How large is the room where the arrangement will be placed?
4. From what point of view will the arrangement be seen: below, at, or above eye-level?
5. Is the arrangement being designed for a specific location?

Examples of good composition:

1. Decorative arrangements should be designed to fit the size of the room. One-sided arrangements are good as they take little space, with all flowers in easy view.
2. Round arrangements are appropriate when the arrangement will be viewed from all sides.
3. A centerpiece for a table will be seen from below eye-level until guests are seated, when it will be at eye-level. It should look good from any angle.
4. An arrangement for a coffee table should be designed all the way around so that it can be viewed from any point in the room.

This vase arrangement of decorative mixed flowers fits the setting it was created for and adds the finishing touch to the tea buffet.

A floral arrangement must be physically and visually balanced. Balance is achieved when a design gives a feeling of stability. This is accomplished by establishing a pattern with the flowers. There are two forms of physical balance: symmetrical and asymmetrical.

In symmetrical balance a vertical line splits the arrangement in half. The two halves may be identical or vary slightly as long as the visual weight of the materials used on each side appear to be equal. The focal point is in the center of the arrangement at the base of the vertical line. An example of a symmetrical arrangement is an equilateral triangle.

In asymmetrical balance the same amount of visual weight appears on each side, but the distance is not equal. The imaginary vertical line has been moved to the right or left of the arrangement's center and the visual weight balanced accordingly. This is often done with a high vertical line on one side and a low horizontal line on the other. An example of an asymmetrical arrangement is a scalene triangle.

Figure 28-1

Figure 28-2

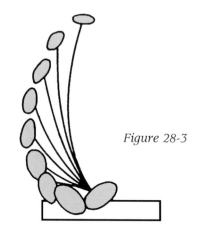

Figure 28-3

There are several ways to visually balance an arrangement.

1. Bilateral symmetry occurs when one side of the arrangement is exactly like the other (Fig. 28-1). Fan-shaped designs are bilaterally symmetrical.
2. Equidimensional symmetry has all points of the design equidistant from the center (Fig. 28-2). Table arrangements are often equidimensionally symmetrical.
3. Spiral symmetry is used in an arrangement such as a garland on a candelabra. The flowers are placed around a center pole or stem so that the stems become shorter as they curve outward, forward, and downward (Fig. 28-3).

Achieving Balance:

1. Dark colors should be used low in the arrangement, as they appear heavy.
2. A small flower appears lighter than a large flower. Large, mass flowers should be grouped lower in the arrangement.
3. Stems should appear to come from a central point in the arrangement.
4. Flower buds, small flowers, and/or pieces of foliage help balance an arrangement. They should be placed at the top and edges of an arrangement, with larger flowers working toward the center.

This symmetrically balanced arrangement is a good example of bilateral symmetry.

Proportion and Scale

This arrangement should be placed on a small table in a delicate room to be in proper proportion and scale.

Proportion is the visual relationship when flowers, foliages, containers, accessories, and space appear comfortable and appropriate together. A good starting point in determining proportion is the standard rule stating an arrangement should be 1 1/2 times the height or width of the container. There are always exceptions to this rule, but in most cases this will give you the proper proportion.

When designing a centerpiece the general rule is that the height of the arrangement should be no higher than 14 inches. However, new styles of design allow exceptions to this rule; certain container styles allow arrangements to be raised above eye-level so that conversation can still flow.

Questions to ask yourself when determining proper scale:

1. What size is the room?
2. How big is the piece of furniture on which the arrangement will be set?
3. If the design is for a party, how many guests will attend?
4. What style is the room decorated in?

Achieving Proportion:

1. The container is the most important part of proportion, as it determines the size and shape of the design, as well as the textures and colors used. In determining proportion the container should be a subordinate part of the total design.
2. Texture helps determine proportion. A container of heavy material carries more visual weight than one of similar size in a more delicate material.
3. Foliage should be of the same classification as the flowers to keep the arrangement in proportion.
4. There are three major areas of the arrangement to look at:
   a. The background forms the longest and strongest lines of the arrangement and often forms the outline.
   b. The middle of the arrangement will be half-opened flowers and smaller flowers of medium size and medium color value. Called the transition area, this is the bridge that leads the eye to the focal area.
   c. The center of interest is usually just above the rim of the container, sometimes breaking the line of the container edge for total unity in the arrangement. Usually the largest flowers and strongest colors are used here.

Rhythm gives the feeling or appearance of motion and carries the eye smoothly through a design. More than any other single factor, it lends distinction to a composition. Good rhythm encompasses spacing, facing, shapes, sizes, and color. It is easier to establish rhythm with an odd number of flowers; however, the important factor is how the flowers are used rather than how many are used.

Achieving Rhythm:

1. Spacing — Good rhythm has gradual but uneven spacing from the focal point (Fig. 30-1). Spaces should be larger at the top and edges of the composition, then become progressively smaller toward the base and center.
2. Facing — Starting at the top of the design, flowers should look upwards and backwards, going to side facing, then to forward facing at the focal point. This will result in smooth, graceful rhythm.
3. Shapes — Related shapes can add character to rhythm. Carnations and scotch broom form a pleasing rhythmic motion, as do roses with eucalyptus, or iris and snapdragons. Facing the flowers in a specific direction will give them an appearance of having a different shape and make a more pleasing rhythm.
4. Sizes — A progression of small to large flowers, such as in a bud vase, is very rhythmic. If the flowers are the same size, foliage can be used to achieve a light and airy feeling on the edge of the arrangement. An illusion of size can be achieved by clustering flowers in groups of various sizes.
5. Color — Color rhythm is achieved several ways: a gradual change of color from one hue to another (yellow to orange), a change in values (light to dark), moving from one value to another (bright, intense to soft, dull). Grouping colors together can produce a very rhythmic look in designs.

Curly willow sweeps through the arrangement, creating rhythm.

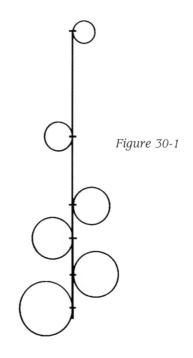

Figure 30-1

Harmony

Harmony deals with intangibles (aesthetic qualities) rather than physical properties. Harmony is that which is pleasing and appealing. A design should create some kind of impression, whether it be beauty, drama, dignity, sweetness, or inspiration. Work on a specific theme for each design by using containers, flowers, and accessories which will provide a total harmony when completed. You will know when harmony has been achieved if you sense complete compatibility among the elements.

Questions to ask yourself before designing for harmony:
1. Do the materials go well together?
2. Do the colors blend pleasingly? If there are contrasts, are they consistent with the theme?
3. Does the container have the same feeling as the arrangement?
4. Do accessories fortify the theme and color of the arrangement?

Examples of good harmony:
1. A crystal or silver container filled with formal flowers such as roses or carnations heightens the elegance of a formal dinner party.
2. A basket filled with spring flowers such as iris, daffodils, tulips, or daisies in mixed colors of yellow, pink, lavender, and blues brings out the gaiety of the Easter and spring season. If they are in coordinated colors, the addition of items such as pussywillow stems, a robin, or a stuffed rabbit enhances the spring theme.
3. Pink or blue flowers such as daisies, sweetheart roses, and miniature carnations are delicate blossoms which represent a new baby. Baby accessories such as rattles express the occasion.
4. The color of turning leaves is echoed in bronze-colored flowers for a centerpiece during the fall and Thanksgiving. A basket or heavy pottery provides the right harmony for the arrangement. Dried materials can be used for accent.
5. A vase of red roses says beauty. The elegant simplicity of the design holds special meaning for anniversary couples.

Achieving Harmony:
1. The lines in the arrangement should originate from a central point. Do not cross stems or march them along in a row (Figs. 31-1, 31-2).
2. Watch for enclosing spaces where 2 lines meet, or seem to meet, at their tips (Fig. 31-3). Space should be open and free.
3. Avoid sharp contrast between sizes, shapes, textures, and colors.
4. Do not let the container become dominant.

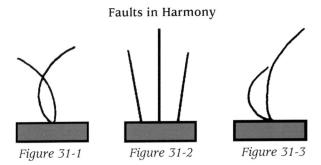

Faults in Harmony

Figure 31-1	*Figure 31-2*	*Figure 31-3*

The crisp, white daisies harmonize with the pewter dinnerware to provide a colonial setting.

Depth occurs when flowers and foliages are distributed around a central point. If all lines are placed like the spokes of a fan, the arrangement will be flat and lack character, but if some lines point backward and some forward, there will be depth. Do not overdo the line direction or the arrangement will appear to tip forward or backward.

Achieving Depth:
1. Look at an arrangement from the side to be sure the lines are neither too long nor too short. Look down on it from above to be sure the lines are going in the right direction.
2. Complete the back of the arrangement to give the appearance of more depth.
3. An illusion of depth can be obtained by using cool, receding colors toward the back of the arrangement.
4. Achieve depth by facing flowers (see page 30). Facing gives depth to an arrangement as the flowers are not at the same angle or closeness to each other.

Line
Lines are the framework around which the rest of the arrangement is built. The framework determines the shape of the arrangement as well as its size. Lines are often suggested by the form of floral materials.

There are several types of line:
1. The vertical line stresses height rather than width. This is a line of strength, force, vigor, power and dignity. It can create a feeling of formality in the proper setting and is like an exclamation point, demanding attention.
2. The horizontal line stresses width instead of height and is placed parallel to the surface. This is a line of peace, quiet, tranquility and slow motion. It suggests sleep and rest.
3. The diagonal line has a slanting or sloping placement. It expresses restlessness, insecurity, and uncertainty. It can be very striking used in combination with vertical or horizontal lines.
4. Curved lines take the same directions as straight lines but are more graceful, appealing and interesting. They express motion, animation, gentleness, and gaiety. They can be used alone or in combination with straight lines.

The gladioli and cylindrical container command a vertical line.

Flowers and foliages of various textures are designed in this arrangement. The yellow lily in the lower half of the arrangement forms the focal point.

Texture refers to the physical surface qualities of flower and foliage materials. It affects the senses of sight and touch. Textures can be rough or smooth, downy or prickly, leathery or satiny, etc.

Achieving Texture:

1. Textures must be related so they blend pleasingly. The textures of the containers and accessories should be in harmony with the texture of the flowers and foliages; otherwise, they can draw attention away from the flowers.
2. Bold, strong contrasts in texture can add interest to an arrangement. Harmony can be achieved by the use of transitional materials with characteristics of both textures.
3. Textures vary in color. Delicate, pastel colors usually have a smooth texture while dark colors suggest a rough texture.

The focal point is the spot in the arrangement that first attracts the eye. The eye starts at this point and travels through the arrangement.

Achieving Focal Point:

1. The main line of the arrangement runs through the focal point. Balance is achieved by the division of materials.
2. The largest flowers, strongest colors, most unusual foliages, or large accessories are usually placed in the focal point area. They should be kept low for stability and appear above the edge of the container.
3. Color is very important. The focal point may be the darkest flower, but it should be only slightly darker than neighboring flowers. If the contrast is too great, the visual motion of the design will be lost.
4. Plan the focal point. If small flowers such as pompon mums will be used, they should be facing upward to pick up the line of the arrangement. Keep the major concentration of flowers in the focal area.
5. Focal point need not always be at the converging lines of an arrangement. The focal area may be the design itself, which fills a special need in its surroundings as a whole, integral unit. A vase of roses is a good example of this.

Ribbon and Bows

Ribbon comes in many sizes and styles, reflecting the current trends of the industry. The most common ribbon sizes are No. 3, No. 9 and No. 40 (Fig. 34-1).

No. 3 is widely used to decorate arrangements, bud vases, planters and 4-inch plants. Commonly used in corsage and wedding work, it is generally available in satin, velvet and lace. No. 9 is used to decorate 6" plants and other items of similar size, as well as presentation bouquets and large arrangements. Lace, satin, velvet and fabric are most common. No. 40 is primarily used for large bows for church decorations and wreaths. This size usually comes in satin, velvet, lace and plastic.

Other ribbon sizes are available for specialized applications. Double-face 1/8 inch and 1/4 inch satin styles are used for delicate arrangements. No.1, generally available in satin only, is 1/2-3/8 inch wide and is used for general decorative accents in arrangements. No. 5 is a common size for specialty ribbon, cotton prints, velvet and lace. Some satins are available, but they are not as widely used.

Figure 34-1 shows bows made of (left to right) No. 40, No. 9 and No. 3 size ribbon.

To Make A Bow

1. Hold ribbon in one hand, gathering it a few inches from the end. Make loop (#1), gathering between the thumb and forefinger (Fig. 35-1).
2. Make loop (#2) on the other side, equal in size and gather in the center (Fig. 35-2).
3. Make loops (#3 and #4) in the same manner (Fig. 35-3).
4. Make loop (#5) and gather. Make a short loop and gather in the center. This becomes the nose of the bow (Fig. 35-4).
5. Make loop (#6) and gather. Check to be sure that the ribbon is facing the right direction after the nose loop is completed.
6. Finish by making loops on each side, until the bow is the desired size (Fig. 35-5).
7. To secure the ribbon, run a wire through the loop in the center of the bow (Fig. 35-6). Pull both ends of the wire together at the back of the bow and pinch tight to the bow with the opposite hand. Twist the two wires together tightly, tying the bow in place.
8. Straighten the loops to make sure the bow is complete (Fig. 35-7).

The types and varieties of ribbon available have expanded in the last several years. Wire-edge ribbon, available in many sizes and materials, is the most popular. The ribbon is manufactured with wire in its side edges, making it easy to bend into the desired shape.

Ribbon and bows can be attractive, but they can also be overdone. Before using them, carefully analyze the design style and occasion.

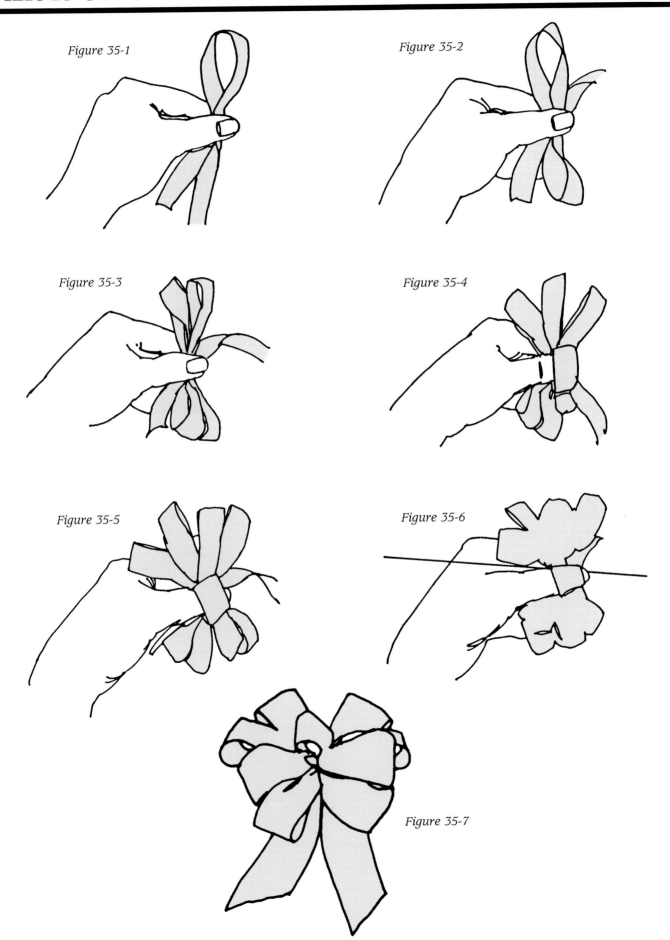

Figure 35-1

Figure 35-2

Figure 35-3

Figure 35-4

Figure 35-5

Figure 35-6

Figure 35-7

Although wiring flowers is not as critical to basic floral design as other techniques, it is important to understand. Wiring is widely used in corsage and wedding designs, but has limited use in arrangements. Flower stem support is the main reason for wiring flowers in floral arrangements. All basic wiring techniques are described in this section.

Wire Weights

Common green enamel florist wire in 18-inch lengths, is available in several gauges, from thick wire No. 18 to fine wire No. 30. Heavy gauge wire is used to support heavier-stemmed flowers. Medium weight wire is used for roses, carnations and other flowers which need firm but not rigid support. Lightweight wire is generally used for delicate flowers like stephanotis or daisies. This type of wire allows for more flexibility in your design work. The best rule for choosing the proper wire weight is to pick the lightest weight which will achieve the amount of support desired.

While you are working, the wire should be kept on hand just in case, in a suitable wire holder. Each wire gauge should be clearly marked with its gauge numbers, so that you can quickly select the proper wire needed.

Paddle wire is also available for floral use in several gauges. Paddle wire is one consecutive length of wire wound onto a bolt. This type of wire is used when longer lengths are needed for the job you are working on.

How To Wire Flowers

There are several basic ways to wire flowers:

1. Twist-Wrap Method — In this method, a wire is inserted into the flower at the base of its head. The flower's stem and wire are twisted together. This method is used only when the design can be made in such a way that the wire is covered or hidden by other flowers and foliage. (Not pictured).

2. Pierce Method — Flowers with a heavy swelling beneath the flower head (roses, carnations) can be wired by piercing. Push one end of the wire through the flower, just above the swollen section (Fig 36-1), using half the length of the wire. Bend both ends down along the stem (Fig 36-2). Tape, starting just above the pierce. (See page 40 for further information on taping.)

3. Insert Method — This method can be used for flowers with the heads firmly fastened to the stem, such as asters. Wire strong enough to hold flower head erect and about six to nine inches long is required. (Some people prefer to use No. 22 wire for this method.) Cut the flower stem to about one inch length. Push the wire along the stem into the flower until it is firm (Fig. 36-3). Tape stem and wire together. For flowers with hollow stems (daffodils, orchids, cornflowers), leave a longer stem of two or three inches; push the wire up through the stem until it seems firm (Fig. 36-4). Tape the stem.

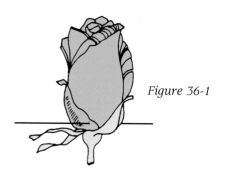

Figure 36-1

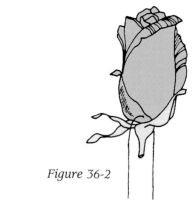

Figure 36-2

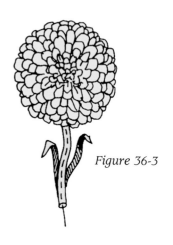

Figure 36-3

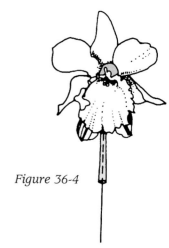

Figure 36-4

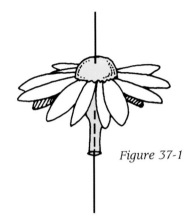

Figure 37-1

4. Hook Method — This method can be used with any flower that has a hard disc-like center (daisies, mums, asters). Push the wire along or through the stem until the wire has poked through the center of the flower about 11/2 inches (Fig. 37-1). Form a hook (Fig. 37-2), and pull the wire gently back down, making sure that the hook is secure in the blossom head and concealed (Fig. 37-3). Tape the stem.

5. Wrap-Around Method — Any flower can be wired with this method, but it is especially effective for flowers placed in small clusters (baby's breath, statice). A No. 26 or No. 28 wire is usually used. Wrap the wire several times around the stem or stems, making sure that clusters are not wrapped so tightly as to appear "bunchy" (Fig. 37-4). Bend the two wires parallel (Fig. 37-5) and tape.

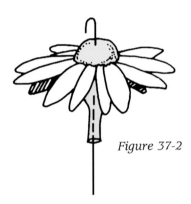

Figure 37-2

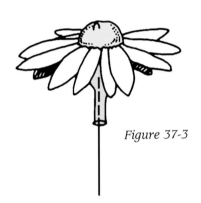

Figure 37-3

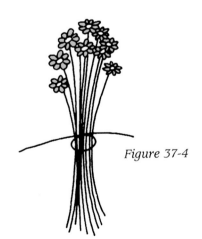

Figure 37-4

Figure 37-5

Wiring Basics

How To Wire Foliage

The use of foliage greatly enhances the appearance of most designs. Properly wired foliage will allow you to utilize varieties whose stems are not strong enough to use on their own or whose mass is not great enough to use without clustering. Wired foliages can be bent or angled to create interesting lines in your arrangement.

There are 3 basic ways to wire foliage.

1. Leaf Form — Pierce a wire through the back of the leaf near the rib (Fig. 38-1). Pierce the wire high enough on the leaf so there will be complete control of the leaf, but not so high that the wire will show in the bouquet. Push the wire halfway through, pull down and tape. (See page 40 for further information on taping.)

2. Cluster Form — Gather the foliage tips in the hand and wrap them together with wire (Fig. 38-2). Tape the stems.

3. Fern Form — Foliages such as leatherleaf (baker fern) and other fronds are wired most effectively with a hairpin. Insert the hairpin through the frond near the top, straddling a rib (Fig. 38-3). Pull down until the bend of the hairpin rests on the fern rib, then tape the wire to the stem.

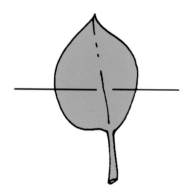

Figure 38-1

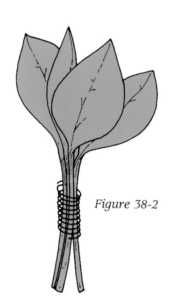

Figure 38-2

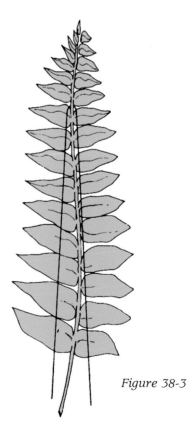

Figure 38-3

Wiring Basics

Special Techniques

Certain flowers may require special wiring techniques. Orchids are one of these flowers. Special orchid stems (green plastic tubes containing cotton-covered wire) have been designed to facilitate the use of orchids or other short-stemmed flowers in arrangements. To use, cut the flower stem on a slant. Insert the top wire into the stem, making sure the extended cotton covers the slant (Fig. 39-1). Slip the green plastic tube over the wire and wick (Fig. 39-2), letting the wick extend to the bottom (Fig. 39-3). Dip the tube in water to start wick action (Fig. 39-4). If needed, the tube can be cut to the desired length. These stems, which keep the flower moist, are excellent for orchids, lilies and similar flowers. These stems save time over the old method of placing a stem in a water tube and staking in an arrangement.

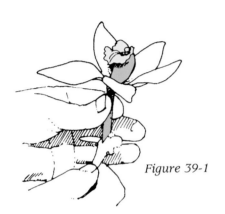

Figure 39-1

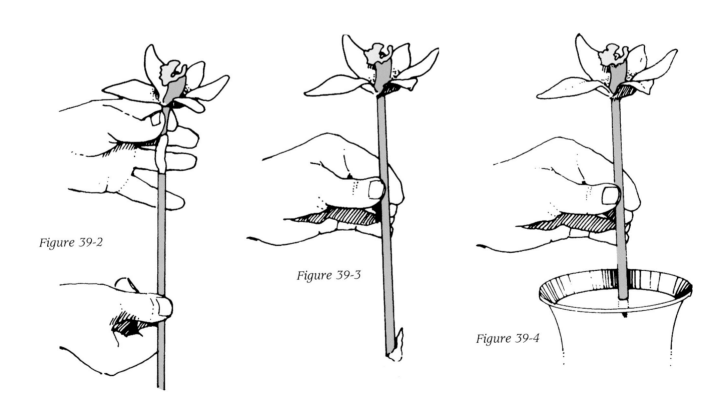

Figure 39-2

Figure 39-3

Figure 39-4

Taping Basics

Flowers wrapped with stem wrap after wiring have a more natural, finished look. A technique usually associated with corsage and wedding design, it also has floral design applications. The mechanics of a flower wired for support can be hidden by tape. Wooden picks can be secured to novelty trims and water tubes with tape for insertion into arrangements.

How To Tape Flowers

1. Stretch, then fold stem wrap around the top of the stem. Pinch it together until it sticks (Fig. 40-1).
2. Stretch the stem wrap as it is wound around stems or wires (Fig. 40-2). Stretching provides a more uniform wrap and helps the stem wrap seal itself.
3. Roll or twirl the stem into the tape while stretching the tape downward with the hand, making a long tight spiral wrap, lapping the edges for complete coverage (Fig. 40-3).
4. Seal the tape by running your fingers down the stem.
5. When the area has been covered, tear the stem wrap off and press to seal the end (Fig. 40-4).

Taping Novelty Trims

To tape wooded picks to flowers or novelty trims, follow the basic taping method listed above. Take care to cover the wooden pick completely to give the trim a finished look. Be cautious not to use too much tape, or the finished stem will take on a bulky appearance. This will probably show and distract from the finished arrangement.

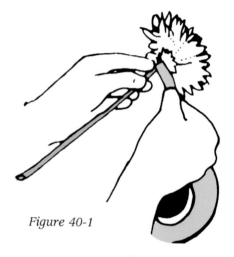

Figure 40-1

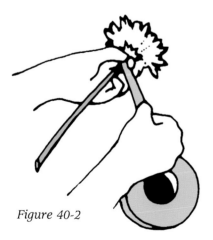

Figure 40-2

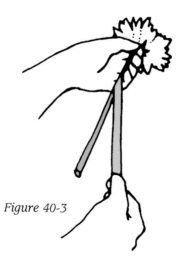

Figure 40-3

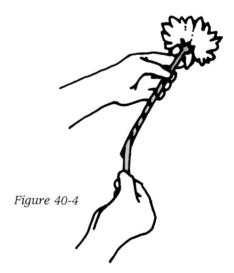

Figure 40-4

Styling Techniques

HOW TO STYLE

Vase
Arrangements

Vase arrangements are flowers loosely arranged in a container, usually designed without mechanical support. There are two common styles of vase arrangements: bud vases for single flowers or smaller designs and larger vases for mixed flowers and/or a dozen arranged flowers. Bud vases and vase arrangements of one type of flower tend to have a more structured design style than larger vases of mixed flowers.

Vase Arrangements

Turn a gift of boxed roses into an elegant floral display. A classic vase arrangement of a dozen long-stem red roses.

Follow the basic steps listed below to create a simple vase arrangement.

Supplies Needed:

1. One vase
2. Mechanical supplies (optional) - chicken wire, tape, floral foam cellophane wrap, needlepoint holder.
3. Flowers - any flower can be used for vase arrangements. Form and mass flowers like roses, carnations, miniature carnations and pompons are attractive in this style. Lilies, gerbera daisies, daffodils, spray orchids, freesia, iris and daisies are other flowers which can provide the right look.
4. Filler flowers (optional) - to soften the look of the vase arrangement. Genista, gypsophila, heather, statice and wax flower are excellent flowers which can accomplish this.
5. Foliages - to help establish a base to design in. Camellia, huckleberrry, leatherleaf, myrtle and salal can be used for this purpose. Other foliages, such as bear grass, Christmas greens, eucalyptus, fern, galax, ming fern, plumosa, scotch broom, sprengeri and tree fern, can also be used to accent a vase arrangement.

Figure 44-1

Preparation:

Method 1:

1. Fill vase with water and floral preservative.
2. Insert base foliage in vase. Use enough foliage to act as an anchor for the flowers (Fig. 44-1).
3. Insert additional foliage as needed when arranging.

Method 2:

1. Cut a piece of chicken wire slightly larger than the opening of the vase selected to be used.
2. Bend wire, insert in opening of vase forming a grid.
3. Tape grid to vase to secure. Add water and floral preservative.

Method 3:

1. Cut soaked floral foam above the rim of the container. Fit snugly into container, leaving approximately 1 inch of foam above the rim of the container.
2. Anchor foam to container with waterproof tape. Add water until foam is submerged.
3. Pre-green container with small pieces of foliage.
4. If using a clear container, pack crushed cellophane loosely around the floral foam to disguise the mechanics.

Figure 44-2

Figure 45-3

Styling the Arrangement:

1. Place primary flower into container to establish height. This should be 1 1/2-2 times the height of the container. Cut each flower stem with a sharp knife as flower is placed in vase.
2. Place additional flowers by inserting them randomly. Work down from the top primary flower to the rim of the vase (Fig. 44-2). For a structured look, be sure to space flowers evenly. If designing a vase to be seen from all sides, be sure flower placement is balanced and round in shape.
3. Insert accent foliage into the design to complement the flowers. Be sure to let the natural foliage of the flowers become part of the design. Remember to remove any flower foliage which will be placed below the water line.
4. If desired, place filler flowers into the arrangement to fill space and help shape arrangement into the desired form. They should not extend above the top flower (Figs. 45-3, 45-4).
5. Evaluate the design; adjust as needed to complete the design (Fig. 45-5).

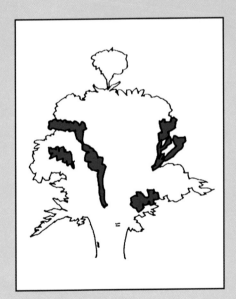

Figure 45-4

Figure 45-5

Pictured to the left, a bud vase of variegated carnations and baby's breath; to the right, a bud vase of lavender roses accented with tree fern.

Follow the basic steps listed below to create simple bud vases like those shown above.

Supplies Needed:

Please refer to this section of page 44. Mechanical supplies will not be needed to create a bud vase design.

Preparation:

1. Fill bud vase with water and preservative.
2. Insert 1 stem of base foliage into opening of prepared vase.

Styling the Bud Vase:

1. Place primary flower into vase to establish height. This should be 1 1/2 times the height of the vase. Cut each flower stem with a sharp knife as flower is placed in vase.
2. Place 1 or 2 additional flowers in vase, working down from the primary flower.
3. Insert accent foliage, if needed, into the design to complement the flowers. Be sure to let the natural foliage of the flowers become part of the design. Remember to remove any flower foliage which will be placed below the water line.
4. Evaluate the design; adjust as needed to complete the design.

Sonia roses arranged with baby's breath in a coordinating vase, perfect for a bridal shower or anniversary gift.

A mixture of spring flowers designed in a glass vase, created to brighten any location.

Design Tips:

1. Often foliage and flowers have been stripped of lower leaves for proper care and handling; however, this can make for an unattractive arrangement in a clear container. Two inches of water in the container will supply sufficient moisture, allowing you to keep foliage on bottom stems. If this technique is used, add water daily to maintain the lower water level.
2. For firmer support, a pin holder "frog" can be inserted into the bottom of the vase to hold the stems in place.
3. Use the natural foliage of flowers whenever possible.
4. Keep it simple. Do not crowd flowers in vase.

Design Ideas:

1. Gladioli and their foliage provide a contemporary look in a tall or round vase.
2. Orchid stems such as dendrobium, oncidiums, cymbidiums and arachnis make a showy and elegant arrangement with only one or two stems. Add accent foliage and the look is complete.
3. Sweetheart roses with filler make an attractive hostess gift.
4. Arrange packaged cash-and-carry bouquets to create exciting vase arrangements. Insert additional flowers or foliage if needed.
5. Rubrum or other styles of lilies create a classic look in a crystal or glass vase.
6. Utilize containers such as glasses, wine carafes and pitchers for interesting designs.
7. Small vases filled with fresh flowers can accent any room, providing a touch of springtime year-round.

HOW TO STYLE

Triangular Arrangements

The popular triangular arrangements
referred to as one-sided and styled
arrangements are forms of the basic
geometric triangles known as
equilateral, right, scalene,
and isosceles.
Although triangular arrangements are
normally viewed from the front, you
must be careful to always create a
proper design which can be
viewed from all sides.

Triangular Arrangements

Red carnations and white pompon chrysanthemums form a simple right triangle accented with eucalyptus.

Follow the basic steps listed below to create a simple triangle arrangement.

Supplies Needed:

1. One container.
2. Floral foam and tape.
3. Primary flowers — to create a central focal point. Form and mass flowers like anthurium, carnations, chrysanthemums, gerbera daisy, iris and roses are flower types which can accomplish this.
4. Secondary flowers — to create interest and unity. They are also used to keep the cost down, as primary flowers tend to be more expensive. Alstroemeria, anemones, asters, bouvardia, miniature carnations, cornflowers, pompon mums, freesia and daisies are flowers which can be used.
5. Filler flowers (optional) — complete the "look" and fill space. Yarrow, statice, heather, gypsophila, astilbe and amaranthus are often used.
6. Foliage — to form a background and reinforce the line of the arrangement. Eucalyptus, fern, leatherleaf, myrtle, palm, ruscus and scotch broom are foliages which can achieve this.

Figure 50-1

Preparation:

1. Cut soaked floral foam to fit snugly into the container, leaving approximately 1 inch of foam above the rim of the container.
2. Anchor foam to container with waterproof tape. Add water.
3. If arrangement is an open design style, cover with moss for a natural look. Less foliage will be needed to pre-green. Sheet, fresh or Spanish moss can be used for this purpose. Fasten moss in place by inserting greening pins through the moss into the floral foam. (This step is optional.)
4. Pre-green the container:
   a. Take 2 stems of foliage. Cut each in half.
   b. Place the top half of both stems back to back. This will form a vertical cone.
   c. Place foliage towards the back of the container.
   d. Insert remaining halves in floral foam to create a triangular outline for the arrangement.
   e. Fill in lightly with foliage to cover any exposed floral foam (Fig. 50-1).
5. Wire any flowers which require additional support (see pages 36-39).

Figure 50-2

Figure 51-1

Styling the Arrangement:

1. Place primary flowers into the container to establish height and width. The first flower should be approximately 1 1/2-2 times the height of the container. The next primary flowers should be placed to establish the width and triangular shape.
2. Place remaining primary flowers into the container. They should be placed for maximum visibility as they help form the focal point of the arrangement (Fig. 50-2).
3. Place secondary flowers into the arrangement. These will form the boundaries of the triangle and complete the arrangement (Fig. 51-1).
4. If desired, place filler flowers into the arrangement to fill space and help shape design into the desired form (Fig. 51-2). Filler flowers should not extend above the top flowers and should be concentrated into the body of the arrangement. Do not "over-stuff" the arrangement.
5. Evaluate the design; adjust as needed to make a triangular shape (Fig. 51-3).

Figure 51-2

Figure 51-3

Blue iris, a mixture of chrysanthemum pompons and statice form a basic triangular arrangement. This arrangement would make a lovely accent for a breakfast nook or casual room setting.

Triangle arrangements are appropriate for many occasions. The simplicity of this design style makes it popular for floral gifts, entertaining and home decoration. A wide variety of flowers can be used in the triangle arrangement style. Larger flower forms can be combined with smaller flowers to create interesting looks. The use of one flower variety can create a dramatic look.

Triangle arrangement styling utilizes four different triangle forms. These basic forms are described in more detail in the Design Tips section on page 53.

Graceful lilies and miniature carnations are arranged in the scalene triangle form. This design style takes more practice than simpler forms of the triangular arrangement style.

Peach gerbera daisies combined with white pompon chrysanthemums create an isosceles triangle.

Design Tips:

1. **Right Triangles:** Flowers are designed in a 90° right angle. A well-styled design should flow high left to low right. To design: establish height with the first flower. Determine length with the low right flower. Focal point is at the low left of the design. The secondary flowers are placed in sculpted fashion to connect height and width. See design featured on page 49.
2. **Isosceles Triangles:** Flowers are designed so two sides are equal and form the height of the arrangement. In this popular arrangement style, height is greater than width, giving the design a slimming look. See design featured on page 53, lower left.
3. **Equilateral Triangles:** Flowers are designed so all three sides are equal. Easy to design, this is a popular style. Flowers should be kept within the triangle for a better design. Focal point should be low in the arrangement. See design featured on page 52.
4. **Scalene Triangles:** Flowers are designed asymmetrically and have a more styled appearance. These arrangements are often designed in compote containers. To design: establish height with first flower. Determine angle and width with lower right flower. Maintain angle and establish the other corner of the triangle with the lower left flower. See design featured on page 53, upper left.

Design Ideas:

1. Add cattails, branches, flowering branches and foliage to extend height of arrangements.
2. Form flowers such as orchids, anthurium and protea work well in right or scalene triangles.
3. Gladioli, snapdragons and liatris add height when needed in a triangular arrangement.
4. Triangles can be designed with only 1 or 2 flower varieties if preferred.
5. Candles create interest in right triangles, especially at Christmas.

HOW TO STYLE

Round Arrangements

Round arrangements, referred to as mounds, colonials or centerpieces, are versatile and can be used for any occasion. In Europe, one style of round arrangement spaces flowers closely together and is called a "Tuzzy Muzzy." The round arrangement is one of the most popular, as it can be viewed from all sides when placed in the center of a table or room.

Round Arrangements

A romantic look is created with yellow sweetheart roses and baby's breath. You can turn a gift of loose flowers into a delicate display, perfect for any location in your home.

Follow the basic steps listed below to create a simple round arrangement.

Supplies Needed:

1. One container.
2. Floral foam and tape.
3. Primary flowers—form and mass types to shape and determine size of arrangement. Round arrangements are often composed of mixed flowers, such as carnations, roses, lilies, iris and tulips.
4. Secondary flowers—to shape arrangement. Generally smaller in size than mass flowers, miniature carnations, pompon mums, daisies and alstroemeria are often used.
5. Filler flowers (optional)—to fill space and complete the "look." Yarrow, statice, gypsophila, heather and astilbe are flowers which can be used for this purpose.
6. Foliage—to help define shape. Leatherleaf, pittosporum, Ming fern, podocarpus, tree fern and Christmas-type greens are foliages which can accomplish this.

Figure 56-1

Preparation:

1. Cut soaked floral foam to fit snugly into the container, leaving approximately 1 inch of foam above the rim of the container.
2. Anchor foam to container with waterproof tape. Add water.
3. If the arrangement is an open design style, cover foam with moss for a natural look. Less foliage will be needed to pre-green. Sheet, fresh or Spanish moss can be used for this purpose. Fasten moss in place by inserting greening pins through the moss into the floral foam. (This step is optional.)
4. Pre-green the container:
   a.   Take 2 stems of foliage. Cut each in half.
   b.   Place the top half of both stems back to back. This will form a vertical cone.
   c.   Place foliage in the center of the container.
   d.   Insert approximately 6 pieces of foliage, all the same length, into floral foam at the rim of the container. Place these pieces an equal distance apart from each other, forming a circle at a right angle to the vertical cone (Fig. 56-1).
   e.   Fill in lightly with foliage to cover any exposed floral foam (Fig. 50-1).
5. Wire any flowers which require additional support (see pages 36-39).

Figure 56-2

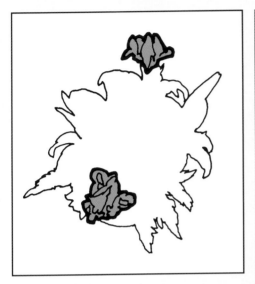

Figure 57-1

Styling the Arrangement:

1. Place primary flowers into the arrangement. Space these throughout the arrangement so that visual interest is evenly distributed and height is established (Fig. 56-2).
2. Insert additional primary flowers into the arrangement for interest and balance (Fig. 57-1).
3. Insert secondary flowers to establish width and define the round shape. All flowers should radiate from the center of the design (Fig. 57-2). Place flowers at different depth levels to create interest.
4. If desired, place filler flowers into the arrangement to fill space and help shape arrangement into the desired form. Filler flowers should not extend above the top flowers and should be concentrated in the body of the arrangement. Do not "over-stuff" the arrangement.
5. Evaluate the design; adjust as needed to make a round shape (Fig. 57-3).

Figure 57-2

Figure 57-3

Round Arrangements

A traditional round arrangement styled with iris, carnations, chrysanthemum pompons and a variety of accent flowers.

The round arrangement style is ideal for utilizing a mixture of flower varieties and colors, and can be used to make a colorful display. Round arrangements can be created in small, delicate formats as well as in large, elaborate stylings. Flowers can be given a tight, compact look or allowed space within the design to create a light, airy feeling.

A feminine arrangement of miniature carnations, freesia, button pompons and tree fern.

Design Tips:

1. Round arrangements do not have a central focal point. The entire arrangement should radiate from the center of the container.
2. Turn the container as you design to get a round effect.
3. If using only one type of flower, place into the arrangement in both primary and secondary positions, as in this style depth creates interest.
4. Foliage can be used as a filler if desired. Tree fern and pittosporum make good filler foliage.

Design Ideas:

1. Use non-fresh items for filler: millimeter balls and pine cones at Christmas, starflowers, yarrow and other dried materials any time, preserved oak leaves and wheat in the fall, novelty trims during holiday periods and latex and micro-mylar balloons for a festive look.
2. For a feminine look, fill a dainty fabric or lace-trimmed basket with sweetheart roses, daisy pompon mums and gypsophila.
3. Design bulb flowers such as daffodils, iris, tulips and grape hyacinth with other flowers for a spring look.
4. Daisies in a basket are always refreshing.
5. For Christmas, use assorted Christmas foliages and pinecones. Accent with a candle.

Mixed fall flowers, here accented with a touch of wheat, create a seasonal look.

HOW TO STYLE
Centerpiece Arrangements

Centerpiece arrangements are the most commonly used decoration for special occasions, and are referred to as long and low or horizontal arrangements.

Often used in the center of a dining room table, centerpieces are designed in pyramidal fashion so that guests have a good view no matter what the angle. They are kept low so that conversation can flow freely across the table. Candles are a common accessory.

Centerpiece Arrangements

White taper candles are in the center of this traditional centerpiece, styled with freesia, miniature carnations, pompon chrysanthemums and statice. Delicate baby's breath adds the finishing touch.

Supplies Needed:

1. One container.
2. Floral foam and tape.
3. Candles (optional)—taper or pillars.
4. Primary flowers—form and mass flowers to shape and determine the size of the arrangement. Centerpieces are often composed of mixed flowers such as carnations, roses, fuji mums, gerbera daisies and lilies.
5. Line flowers—used to establish the length of the design. Stock, snapdragons, spray orchids, liatris, and gladioli are flowers which can achieve this.
6. Secondary flowers—to complete the design. Alstroemeria, miniature carnations, pompon mums, freesia, and daisies are excellent flowers for this purpose.
7. Filler flowers (optional)—fill space and complete the "look" with yarrow, statice, gypsophila, heather, genista and astilbe.
8. Foliage—to help form the long, low shape, insert Christmas greens, eucalyptus, fern, flax, leatherleaf, myrtle and sprengeri.

Figure 62-1

Preparation:

1. Cut soaked floral foam to fit snugly into container, leaving approximately 1 inch of foam above the rim of the container.
2. Anchor foam to container with waterproof tape. Add water.
3. If arrangement is an open design style, cover with moss for a natural look. Less foliage will be needed to pre-green. Sheet, fresh or Spanish moss can be used for this purpose. Fasten moss in place by inserting greening pins through the moss into the floral foam. (This step is optional.)
4. Pre-green the container:
   a. Take 2 stems of foliage. Cut each in half.
   b. Place the top half of both stems back to back. This will form a vertical cone.
   c. Place foliage in the center of the container.
   d. Insert additional whole stems of foliage into the foam on each side of the container to form the length of the centerpiece.
   e. Fill in lightly with foliage to cover any exposed floral foam (Fig. 62-1).
5. Wire any flowers which require additional support (see pages 36-39).

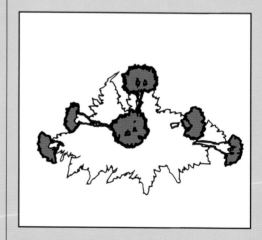

Figure 62-2

Styling the Arrangement:

1. Place a primary line flower on each end of the arrangement to determine its length. Place one flower in the center of the container approximately 1 1/2 times the height of the container to establish height (Fig. 62-2). Place primary flowers on each side to establish width.

2. Insert additional primary flowers into the arrangement. There should be space throughout so that visual interest is evenly distributed (Fig. 63-1).

3. Place secondary flowers to define shape and complete the design. All flowers should appear to radiate from the center of the container (see page 28). Place flowers at different depth levels to create interest.

4. If desired, place filler flowers into the arrangement to fill space and help shape the centerpiece into the desired form. Filler flowers should not extend above the top flowers and should be concentrated in the body of the arrangement (Fig. 63-2). Do not "overstuff" the arrangement.

5. Evaluate the design; adjust as needed to make a pyramidal shape (Fig. 63-3).

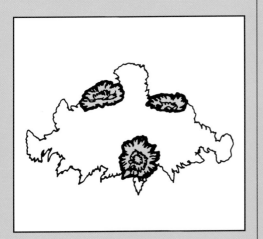

Figure 63-1

Figure 63-2

Figure 63-3

Centerpiece Arrangements

A white pillar candle is featured in this centerpiece style arrangement with holiday appeal.

Centerpieces, like round arrangements, are ideal for creating a multiple flower look. The centerpiece also accommodates styles utilizing 1 or 2 flower varieties only or simple color combinations. A popular design technique of the centerpiece style is to use several flower varieties in the same color range. For instance, an arrangement created with a variety of white flowers can be most attractive.

Design Tips:

1. When designing, keep in mind that since most people will look down into the design, depth is very important.
2. Candle holders can be used to insert and stabilize candles in the arrangement.

Design Ideas:

1. Use pinecones, bows, and millimeter balls in Christmas centerpieces in place of flowers.
2. Centerpieces can be designed to place on mantels for Christmas or for a home wedding.
3. Christmas greens alone make a lasting centerpiece. Fresh flowers can be added for an extra touch and removed when they have wilted.
4. Create simple versions of the basic centerpiece and place on your dining room table on a regular basis.

Red carnations and chrysanthemum pompons are styled into a traditional centerpiece. This flower combination is popular, as both varieties are long-lasting when watered regularly.

HOW TO STYLE

European Style Arrangements

There are four distinct European arrangement styles. Hand-tied bouquets are designed in the hand and can easily be placed in a vase. The clustering technique showcases the individual flower varieties. Vegetative designs have a natural feel. Parallel arrangements show a structured modern feeling.

While each style is unique, together the European style arrangement represents a major force in contemporary floral design.

European Style Arrangements

This design, created in snapdragons, star gazer lilies, chrysanthemum pompons and miniature carnations, represents in its simplest form a parallel style arrangement.

Hand-Tied Bouquets

Hand-tied bouquets are designed to be easily inserted in a vase.

Hand-tied bouquets are designed by shaping the arrangement while holding it, tying it after the design is completed.

Follow the basic steps listed below to create a simple hand-tied bouquet.

How To Style Hand-Tied Bouquets

1. To design, start with a variety of flowers laid out on a table.
2. Start with flowers that have a vertical line; add a few stems of foliage to form the center. All stems must be parallel and should not cross.
3. Hold flowers about 2/3 of the way down the stems; foliage should be stripped below this point. Continue to add flowers, turning the bouquet as they are added. Flower stems should form a spindle effect in the core (Fig. 68-1).
4. Hold stems gently but firmly, making sure that the flowers are evenly distributed to achieve the proper balance (Fig. 68-2).
5. Through experience, the "feel" of the bouquet in your hand will tell you when the bouquet is balanced. Tie off the bouquet with string or raffia around the stems at the point where your hand holds the flowers (Fig. 69-1).
6. Cut stems evenly on the bottom. The arrangement should stand freely on the table (Fig. 69-2).

Styling the other three types of European style arrangements is similar to techniques previously mentioned in other sections. Here we will only describe the styles.

Figure 68-1

Figure 68-2

Figure 69-1

Figure 69-2

Clustering Technique

Clustering of flowers and/or color is an important element of European design. It provides more visual impact to the flowers, especially small flowers which could be buried in a design. Clustering is achieved by using the same variety of flower in a specific section of the design (see arrangement on page 70). This technique lends more importance to the flower. Rather than scattering carnations throughout the design to form shape and style, they might be placed on the left side of the arrangement only. This is a simple technique to employ.

Vegetative Technique

This approach to design provides a natural look to arrangements (see arrangement on page 71, lower left). The arrangement is designed to make the flowers look as if they are growing; the design simulates a natural habitat. Twigs, moss and other woodland touches are used to help establish the live, growing feeling. Garden varieties of flowers such as roses, bulb flowers, anemones, asters, cornflowers, delphinium, liatris, lilies, daisies and snapdragons are often used. Natural flower foliage or foliage that has a natural look is used for this style. Bear grass, fern, and ivy are foliages which can achieve this.

Parallel Technique

This crisp, clean style is not for everyone since it is very geometric and has a contemporary feel. Two or more groupings of flowers are used in a repeated vertical pattern with space between each vertical grouping (see arrangement on page 67). Balance is provided by using at least two groupings. Clustering is very common in this style. Each vertical grouping is generally one variety of flower. Parallel arrangements can also be created by making the same vertical grouping in several varieties and repeating the groupings.

A clustered style arrangement featuring roses, carnations, liatris and miniature carnations.

Understanding the basic forms of European design will allow you to create elegant floral displays using the simplest techniques. Color, flower grouping and natural simplicity are key ideas to remember when designing in European style. Every flower and foliage stem has a reason for being in the design; each contributes to the design's final look.

This hand-tied bouquet is created with a variety of mixed flowers, including snapdragons, alstroemeria, carnations, miniature carnations and iris.

Design Tips:

1. The simplicity of European design is striking because the designs are kept loose and uncluttered, leaving the beauty of each flower and leaf free to be noticed. Design with space in mind; leave ample room around each flower and leaf.
2. One way to achieve a light and airy feel to bouquets is to use fewer flowers than usual. Try replacing three medium-sized flowers, such as carnations, with a single large flower, such as a gerbera daisy. Use less filler material and fill in spaces with interesting and decorative foliage. Mosses can also be used to fill up space and create interest in arrangements.

Design Ideas:

1. Hand-tied bouquets are an excellent way to design a simple bunch of flowers at home. Start with a pre-made bunch and add other flowers as needed.
2. Vegetative designs using bulb flowers are particularly nice in the spring.

A vegetative design focuses on the natural beauty of the flowers. This bouquet features iris, freesia, miniature carnations and lily of the valley. A natural branch adds to the creative appeal of the design.

HOW TO STYLE
Oriental Arrangements

Oriental style arrangements are an important aspect of floral design. Greatly influenced by the exacting art of Ikebana, this style is most often used as an accessory look in the home. Oriental arrangements generally utilize open space and blend nature into the design. The classic elements of heaven, man and earth give the Oriental arrangement a feeling of peacefulness and expressive motion.

Oriental Arrangements

Gerbera daisies form 2 or 3 lines, essential in basic oriental design.
Aspidistra forms the third, the earth line. The rocks provide a tranquil
element, giving the design a feeling of peacefulness and openness.

Follow the basic steps listed below to create a simple oriental arrangement.

Supplies Needed:

1. One low container.
2. Floral foam and tape or pin holder and clay adhesive.
3. Primary flowers with an oriental feel — to create interest. They are usually form flowers, such as alliums, asters, fuji mums, dahlia, gerbera daisies, iris, lilies, and orchids.
4. Line flowers — used to establish the three basic lines of heaven, man and earth. Flowering branches, bare branches and form flowers are most often used.
5. Secondary flowers — used as the "meadow" and "helpers" in oriental design. Smaller than primary flowers, carnations, miniature carnations, cornflowers, pompon mums, ranunculus, and roses are flowers which can be used.
6. Foliage — usually defines the three basic lines and is used sparingly. Natural foliage from the flowers is utilized whenever possible. Flax, ivy, Ming fern, eucalyptus, ti leaves and pittosporum are good foliages to achieve this style.

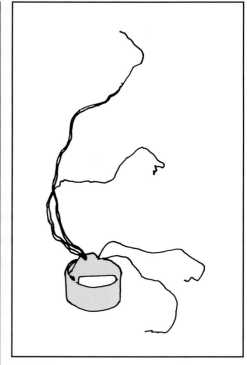

Figure 74-1

Preparation:

1. Cut soaked floral foam to fit snugly in container, leaving approximately 1 inch of foam above the rim of the container. If using a pin holder, anchor it into the container firmly with clay adhesive or hot glue.
2. Anchor foam to container with waterproof tape. Be sure tape does not show.
3. If desired, cover the floral foam with moss for a natural look. Sheet, fresh or Spanish moss can be used for this purpose. Fasten moss in place by inserting greening pins through the moss into the floral foam.
4. Wire any flowers which require additional support (see page 36-39).

Figure 75-1

Styling the Arrangement:

1. Insert 3 primary flowers, line flowers, branches or foliage into the container. Establish the three basic lines of oriental design. This should form an asymmetrical triangle (Fig 74-1).

   a) Heaven, the tallest, is generally 1 1/2-3 times the height of the container.

   b) Man is generally 2/3 the height of heaven. The flower is generally placed directly behind heaven, at a greater angle of inclination.

   c) Earth is generally 1/3-1/2 the height of man and is often placed on the opposite side of heaven and man. It can face upwards or downwards.

2. Place secondary flowers (called mountains and meadows) into the design within the framework of the triangle (Fig 75-1). These enforce the shape and provide a focal point.

3. "Helpers," usually secondary flowers or foliage, are placed to complete the arrangement (Fig. 75-2).

4. Evaluate the design; adjust as needed to make desired shape (Fig. 75-3).

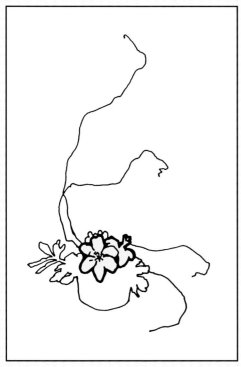

Figure 75-2

Figure 75-3

Bare branches establish the three oriental lines. Cymbidium orchids form the focal point of this classic oriental style.

Oriental design is an expressive form of floral design. All elements of the design have meaning and are important to the final creation. Simplicity is the key feeling of most oriental design. When created in its true spirit, the oriental design becomes an elegant art form.

Gerbera daisies and carnations form an expressive line.

Design Tips:

1. Openness is the key to this style: less is more.
2. Use only one or two varieties of flowers for an optimum look.
3. Utilize foliage, flowering branches and dried materials to carry out the theme.

Design Ideas:

1. Fully open gladioli are spectacular in a low bowl design.
2. Combine seasonal elements which are very oriental in feeling.
   a. Winter — Bare branches.
   b. Spring — Pussy willows or flowering branches with bulb flowers.
   c. Summer — Grasses and reeds (like flax) with dahlias.
   d. Fall — Dried materials with chrysanthemums.
3. Use pebbles to add interest in low bowl designs.

The lily, used in its natural state, reaches for heaven. The use of moss and a monkey pod placed low in the container gives this design a feeling of nature.